THE BAHAMAS
ABACO
PORTS OF CALL & ANCHORAGES

BY

THOMAS A. HENSCHEL

AERIAL PHOTOGRAPHY BY

LUCIEN F. MINER

PUBLISHED BY MILE HIGH PUBLISHING & Graphics • WAYNESVILLE • NORTH CAROLINA
DISTRIBUTED BY CRUISING GUIDE PUBLICATIONS, INC. • DUNEDIN • FLORIDA

North Man-O-War Channel

PUBLISHED BY

Mile High Publishing & Graphics
P.O. Box 942 • Waynesville, NC 28786
E-Mail: thlp@earthlink.net
www.abacobound.com

DISTRIBUTED BY

Cruising Guide Publications, Inc.
P.O. Box 1017
Dunedin, Florida 34697-107
Phone: (800) 330-9542 • (727) 733-5322 • Fax: • (727) 734-8179
Web Site: www.cruisingguides.com • E-Mail: info@cruisingguides.com

By Thomas A. Henschel
Publisher

ASSOCIATE PUBLISHER
Lee Marie Whitney

EDITORS
Simon Charles • Judith N. Fannin

AERIAL PHOTOGRAPHY
Lucien F. Miner

SHORESIDE PHOTOGRAPHY
Kathy Find

DEDICATION
To my father, Lester, who instilled in me a lifelong love for the water and outdoors.
To my brother, John, with whom I enjoyed many fine times both on and off the water.
All these times were short-lived.

First Edition
ISBN 0-9704068-0-0

CONTENTS

Kathy Find

ATLANTIC OCEAN

Walker's Cay   Grand Cays

LITTLE BAHAMA BANK

Carters Cays
Moraine Cay

Allans - Pensacola Cay
Spanish Cay
Powell Cay

Great Sale Cay

Manjack Cay
Green Turtle Cay

LITTLE ABACO

Mangrove Cay

Whale Cay
Great Guana Cay

West End

Man-O-War
Cay

Grand Bahama Island

GREAT ABACO

Elbow
Cay
Tilloo
Cay

Freeport

Deep Water Cay

Lynyard Cay

GULF STREAM

Little
Harbour

Mores
Island

Cherokee

CHEROKEE
SOUND

Gorda Cay

Sandy Point

Hole In The Wall

ABACO & THE LITTLE BAHAMA BANK

INTRODUCTION

Abaco has a history that dates back into the 1700's when groups of British loyalists left America to seek out a new life in the islands of the Bahamas. However, it has only been in recent years that Abaco has been rediscovered., namely by cruising boaters, fishermen, divers and vacationers.

While longtime visitors may lament days gone by in Abaco when anchorages were less crowded and marina reservations were never needed, the transition has been inevitable.

Combine a group of spectacularly beautiful islands with protected and easily navigable waters, and you are bound to draw attention. In recent years, Abaco has experienced unprecedented growth and more visitors than ever.

This all has a positive note. Services for cruising boaters have never been better, and the marina facilities often rival or exceed those stateside. Water, ice and fuel is always available, while in the not too distant past, these were always concerns.

Best of all, the residents and business owners of Abaco are the most helpful

Continued on Page 9

Lubbers Quarters Passage

Continued from Page 7

and obliging that you will ever find.

Abaco is comprised of a 100 or so islands and cays, with the major islands of this archipelago being Great Abaco and Little Abaco. Stretching from the northernmost island, Walker's Cay to Hole-In-The-Wall at the southern tip of Great Abaco Island, the waters are largely protected without lengthy bluewater passages. Navigation throughout Abaco is relatively simple, and you are seldom out of sight of another neighboring cay.

The Abaco chain truly seems to have been created for the cruising boater.

The northern reaches of Abaco provide remote and secluded anchorages where you will often find a cay to yourself. Deserted beaches and endless gunkholing possibilities abound. The fishing is outstanding, and the surrounding scenery spectacular. Nonetheless, you are always within hours away from a marina, or settlement.

To the south lies Green Turtle Cay, a favorite port of call for everyone visiting Abaco. This cay offers excellent marinas and anchorages. New Plymouth with its charm and history, is not to be missed.

Treasure Cay Hotel Resort and Marina on the Great Abaco mainland is famed for its world renown beach, and has the only golf course in Abaco.

The Hub of Abaco is comprised of Marsh Harbour and the surrounding outlying islands. Marsh Harbour is the third largest city in the Bahamas after Nassau and Freeport. With a wealth of restaurants, marinas, supplies and services, much of Abaco's cruising activities revolve around Marsh Harbour.

Nearby, Great Guana is a beachcomber's paradise. Miles of remarkably beautiful beaches line both the ocean and Sea of Abaco shores. The settlement provides lodging, restaurants and entertainment.

Neighboring Man-O-War Cay is one of the most interesting communities in Abaco. Here, the local industry is centered around boat building, and has for many years. The industrious character of the residents of this cay is reflected in the neatly kept homes and property.

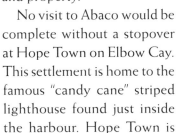

No visit to Abaco would be complete without a stopover at Hope Town on Elbow Cay. This settlement is home to the famous "candy cane" striped lighthouse found just inside the harbour. Hope Town is steeped in history and is the post card village of Abaco.

Further south are some of Abaco's best diving and snorkeling in the Pelican Cays Land and Sea Park. This area has been set aside as a preserve where no fishing or spearfishing is allowed. The park waters teem with fish and undersea life.

Anchorages are again more remote in this area. Among the favorites is Little Harbour, best known for the Johnston's Gallery and Foundry along with Pete's Pub.

Sandy Point lies at the southernmost point of Great Abaco Island, and is known for outstanding bonefishing.

Besides its fame as a cruising grounds, in recent years Abaco offshore waters have gained a reputation for world-class fishing. Marlin tournaments are staged from Abaco Beach Resort and Boat

A "shellular phone" at Pete's Pub. Call anywhere free!

Harbour, Treasure Cay Marina and the Green Turtle Club. These events draw hundreds of top-notch anglers, their boats and crews.

Abaco is a magical cruising destination offering the widest spectrum of activities and sights. Once you have visited Abaco, you are sure to return.

Editor's Note: This book is designed to be used in conjunction and to compliment the several fine guides on Abaco and the Bahamas. These guides and the appropriate nautical charts are essential to safely cruising these islands.

A historic New Plymouth home.
by Kathy Find

Man-O-War Settlement Harbour

Dolphin on the Little Bahama Bank.
by Kathy Find

WEST END, GRAND BAHAMA ISLAND

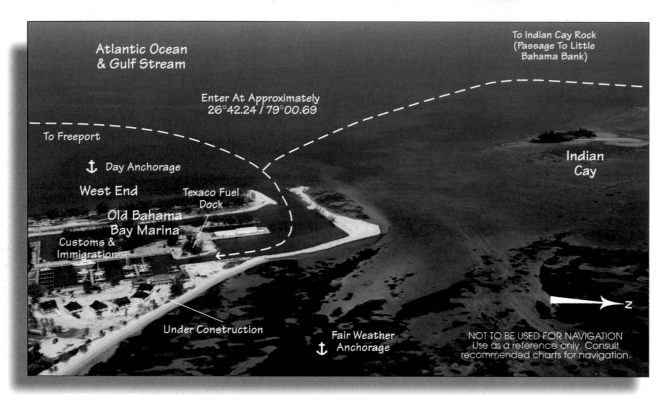

Atlantic Ocean
& Gulf Stream

To Indian Cay Rock
(Passage To Little
Bahama Bank)

Enter At Approximately
26°42.24 / 79°00.69

To Freeport

⚓ Day Anchorage

Indian
Cay

West End   Texaco Fuel
                  Dock

Old Bahama
Bay Marina

Customs &
Immigration

Under Construction

⚓ Fair Weather
   Anchorage

N → Z

NOT TO BE USED FOR NAVIGATION
Use as a reference only. Consult
recommended charts for navigation.

While technically not a part of the Abaco chain of islands proper, West End on Grand Bahama Island, has been included as a destination in this book because it is one of the most popular ports of call when traveling to and from Abaco. Located just over 50 miles from Florida shores, West End is the most convenient stop-over for clearing customs and immigration into the Bahamas after crossing the ocean waters of the Gulf Stream.

NAVIGATION

There are many excellent articles in Bahamas cruising guides that offer helpful information for crossing the Gulf Stream. The best advice, if you are uncomfortable going it alone, is to buddy up with another boat or group of boats headed in the same direction. During the cruising season this is usually a simple matter from any major Florida departure point.

After crossing the Gulf Stream, West End can be spotted by a high tower and a large water tank. The entrance to the Old Bahama Bay Marina is located at the very tip of the island. It is marked with red and green flasher markers, and the approach is straightforward with depths exceeding 15 feet. Once inside, another set of markers will lead you around a breakwater and then into the main basin where the fuel dock is immediately to starboard.

For passage through the Indian Cay Channel, consult your recommended charts and guides.

Anchoring is possible around the northern tip of the island in depths of 6-10 feet, but this should only be considered in fair weather since the area is largely exposed.

ASHORE

Once known as the Jack Tar Marina, the newly remodeled marina is now the Old Bahama Bay Marina. In the past, Jar Tar was one of the largest resorts in the Bahamas. Over the years it fell into disrepair along with the marina, and the old hotel and buildings were torn down some time ago. The new marina is one of the first phases in the development of a resort and residential community called Old Bahama Bay.

Within the marina you will find showers, Bahamas Customs and Immigration, marina office with a lounge area and a property sales office. All of the docks have been redone and future plans call for a restaurant with an indoor-outdoor bar. A regularly scheduled bus service provides inexpensive transportation to nearby Freeport, or taxis are available.

A small settlement is located nearby where a limited selection of groceries and drinks can be purchased for on-board supplies.

GREAT SALE CAY

NOT TO BE USED FOR NAVIGATION
Use as a reference only. Consult
recommended charts for navigation.

anchorage still offers the best protection in the area.

ASHORE

The island offers little in the way of exploration or scenery since it consists largely of mangroves and marsh.

You can land a dingy along the narrow beach and there are ruins of an old U.S. missile tracking station found just inland of the beach. Inside the harbour, you can explore the grassy flats and the mangrove-lined shoreline, or try for bonefish on the surrounding flats.

Another anchorage, Tom Johnson's Harbour, is located on the other side of Great Sale. This may represent an alternative for cruisers traveling from southern Abaco. This anchorage does offer sanctuary from strong west and southwest winds, but is exposed from the east and south. The waters are fairly shallow in this area.

The beauty of Great Sale Cay is that the island's anchorages represents one of the most convenient stop-over points between West End and the popular cruising destinations of southern Abaco.

Great Sale, an uninhabited cay, is low and flat stretching about five miles from north to south. Approaching from the east, the harbour is found at the southern end of the island. A narrow beach flanks the cay for much of its length. The naturally-formed harbour entrance is located at the end of this beach.

NAVIGATION

The anchorage is easily entered. However, give the point off the southeastern shore plenty of room while rounding as there are shoals which extend off the point. Once inside, favor the eastern shore where the water is the deepest. The western side of the harbour shoals to 3 or 4 feet over grassy flats. Generally, all the way up into the northern reaches of the harbour, you will find good holding in several feet of water.

The anchorage provides good protection from most winds, especially strong northers. Blows from the south or southwest can make it a bit uncomfortable, but the

Another view of Great Sale Cay from the southeast showing anchorages on either side of the island.

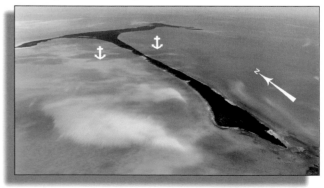

WALKER'S CAY

Shoals

To Channel Entrance From
Little Bahama Bank

Shoals

To Tom Brown's Cay
And Grand Cays

Airstrip

Marina

Coral Heads

Rocks

To Atlantic Ocean

NOT TO BE USED FOR NAVIGATION
Use as a reference only. Consult
recommended charts for navigation.

Mention Walker's Cay to anyone familiar with the Bahamas, and you are likely to end up in a conversation about blue marlin fishing and angling tournaments. Walker's has long been a sportfishing mecca with marlin, tuna, sailfish and wahoo among the favored game.

In recent years, Walker's has also become recognized as a noted diving destination. Shark encounters offered by the dive shop are one of the attractions of diving in the surrounding waters.

NAVIGATION

Walker's Cay is the northernmost of the Bahama Islands and is reached from Florida by crossing the Little Bahama Bank. Most boats from southern Florida destinations will utilize the Indian Cay Channel near West End. For others traveling from departure points, such as Stuart, a more northerly passage may be considered. An example would be just north of Memory Rock. Approaching the island, there are numerous sand banks, and the entrance to the channel leading to Walker's is found just to the east of Tea Table Cay. The

channel is entered on a course of 20° M from Triangle Rocks. The 250-foot tower on the southern end of Walker's will be visible on this heading, and the staked channel carries a depth of approximately 5 feet MLW.

ASHORE

Walker's Cay is a port of entry for Bahamas Customs and Immigration. The full-service marina provides 75 slips in a well-protected horseshoe-shaped basin. It is always best to phone ahead before making the trek to Walker's. During tournament times, it is not uncommon to find the marina and other shoreside facilities booked to capacity. A paved runway serves private planes, and regularly scheduled air service is provided by the management.

Situated on a high bluff, the views of the ocean and surrounding flats are spectacular from the main building of the hotel. The hotel provides excellent restaurants, lounges and two pools. There are beaches located a short walk from the hotel. Besides the hotel accommodations, luxury villas are also available.

Fishing guides and charters are found at the marina, as well as a dive shop which offers ocean outings. While Walker's Cay is largely known for its outstanding offshore fishing, there is great angling on the flats for bonefish and permit. Likewise, reef fishing is extremely productive. Day or overnight trips from Walker's to nearby Grand Cays or Double Breasted Cays are an interesting break from the fishing or diving action.

GRAND CAYS

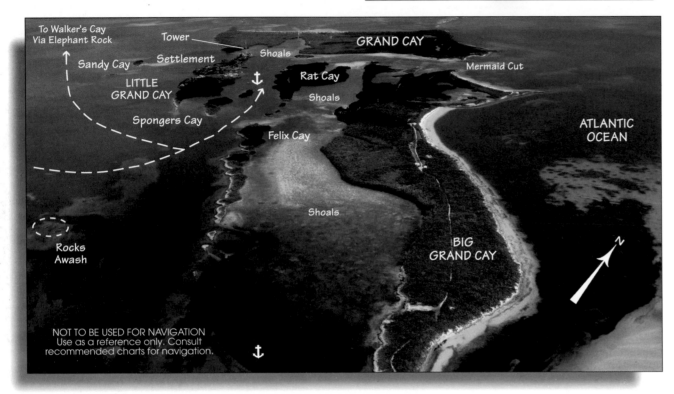

To Walker's Cay
Via Elephant Rock

Tower

GRAND CAY

Sandy Cay   Settlement   Shoals

Mermaid Cut

Rat Cay

LITTLE
GRAND CAY

Shoals

Spongers Cay

ATLANTIC
OCEAN

Felix Cay

Shoals

Rocks
Awash

BIG
GRAND CAY

NOT TO BE USED FOR NAVIGATION
Use as a reference only. Consult
recommended charts for navigation.

The settlement at Little Grand Cay is a laid-back community of a couple hundred residents, most of whom work at neighboring Walker's Cay or are fishermen. The anchorage is located in a well-protected harbour with good holding.

NAVIGATION

A tall telephone communications tower and a water tank provide landmarks to identify Little Grand Cay. The harbour entrance is found at the southwestern tip of the cay and the western shore of Felix Cay. Rocky shoals are usually visible just to the south of Felix Cay. Leave these shoals to starboard while entering the channel. The channel provides depths of about 6 feet MLW.

Rounding the tip of Little Grand Cay, you will keep two other smaller islands to port. The deeper water of the channel is clearly visible. Stay to starboard.

Upon entering the harbour, favor the southern portions for anchoring. Towards the northwest, the water shoals, and you may find yourself high and dry at low tide.

For the passage to Walker's Cay to or from the

harbour around Elephant Rock, consult your charts and guides. There is a small boat channel rounding the northwest tip of Little Grand Cay, but it is only suited for dinghies and outboard skiffs.

Another good anchorage is located between Felix Cay and Big Grand Cay. When entering this anchorage, beware of the aforementioned shoals extending off the southwest tip of Felix Cay.

ASHORE

Dockage is very limited at the settlement. It may be possible to find available slips at Rosie's Place, where fuel is sold. Rosie's features a bar where many of the local residents gather, as well as visiting cruisers and fishermen. They serve excellent Bahamian-style food. The adjoining Island Bay Motel offers air-conditioned accommodations.

A walking tour of the island is interesting. There are paths leading to high bluffs overlooking the ocean and surrounding flats. There are also secluded beaches. Groceries and bakery goods are available at several small stores and shops. Other small restaurants are scattered throughout the community. Everyone is friendly, and the atmosphere is truly the Bahamas.

A major attraction of the Grand Cays area is the light tackle fishing prospects on the flats. The bonefishing is reportedly exceptional.

With a dinghy or small skiff, there are many areas to explore, including the nearby Double Breasted Cays.

DOUBLE BREASTED CAYS

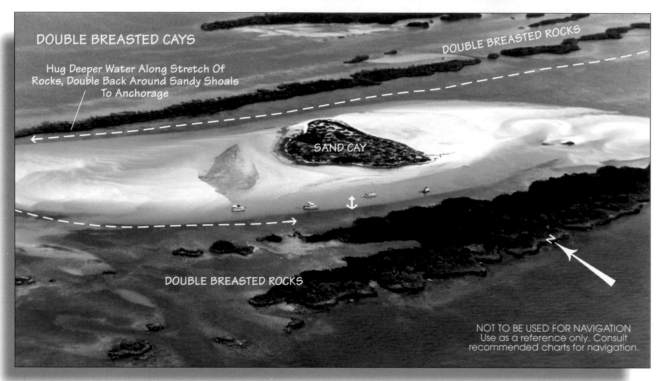

DOUBLE BREASTED CAYS

Hug Deeper Water Along Stretch Of
Rocks, Double Back Around Sandy Shoals
To Anchorage

DOUBLE BREASTED ROCKS

SAND CAY

DOUBLE BREASTED ROCKS

NOT TO BE USED FOR NAVIGATION
Use as a reference only. Consult
recommended charts for navigation.

The picture-perfect anchorages of Double Breasted Cays are popular for their scenery, beaches and remoteness. An incredible spectrum of water colors and many deserted small cays make this archipelago ideal for cruising and exploration. Likewise, the anchorages provide above-average shelter from winds out of most directions.

NAVIGATION

There are a number of anchorages within this group of cays. By far the easiest spot to anchor is just off the southeast section of Double Breasted Rocks. Here you can anchor with good holding in 10-15 feet of water without testing your skills by winding your way into the cays. The drawback of this anchorage is that you are exposed from the south and southwest. From here, you can explore the inner cays by dinghy. You may want to do this in any case if you are unfamiliar with the anchorage in the inner reaches of the cays.

To reach the anchorage pictured, you must follow a northwesterly course along Double Breasted Rocks, leaving the reef, sandbars and Sand Cay to your port. After reaching the end of the chain of rocks, you then swing around on a southerly heading rounding Sand Cay and the surrounding shoals. While navigation is not especially difficult reaching this anchorage, make sure you are comfortable reading the water depths. It is best to enter in only favorable light conditions, and keep in mind the tide flow may be an influence. Tidal flow has carved out these rocks, and it may be especially strong at times, so entering at slack high water may be an option to consider.

The anchorage is also possible to enter from the ocean. There is adequate water depths for most vessels, however, beware of coral heads found in the shallower water nearing the entrance to the anchorage.

Once inside, you are likely to have company as this is an especially popular spot. Be prepared to utilize two anchors, and expect considerable current.

Other protected anchorages can be found at the southern end of Double Breasted Rocks between Double Breasted Cays.

ASHORE

While totally deserted, this group of rocks and cays can provide hours of exploration. The sandy shoals are ideal for swimming, setting out beach chairs, and lounging in an unforgettable setting.

There is extraordinary snorkeling around the many rocks and the fishing is also productive.

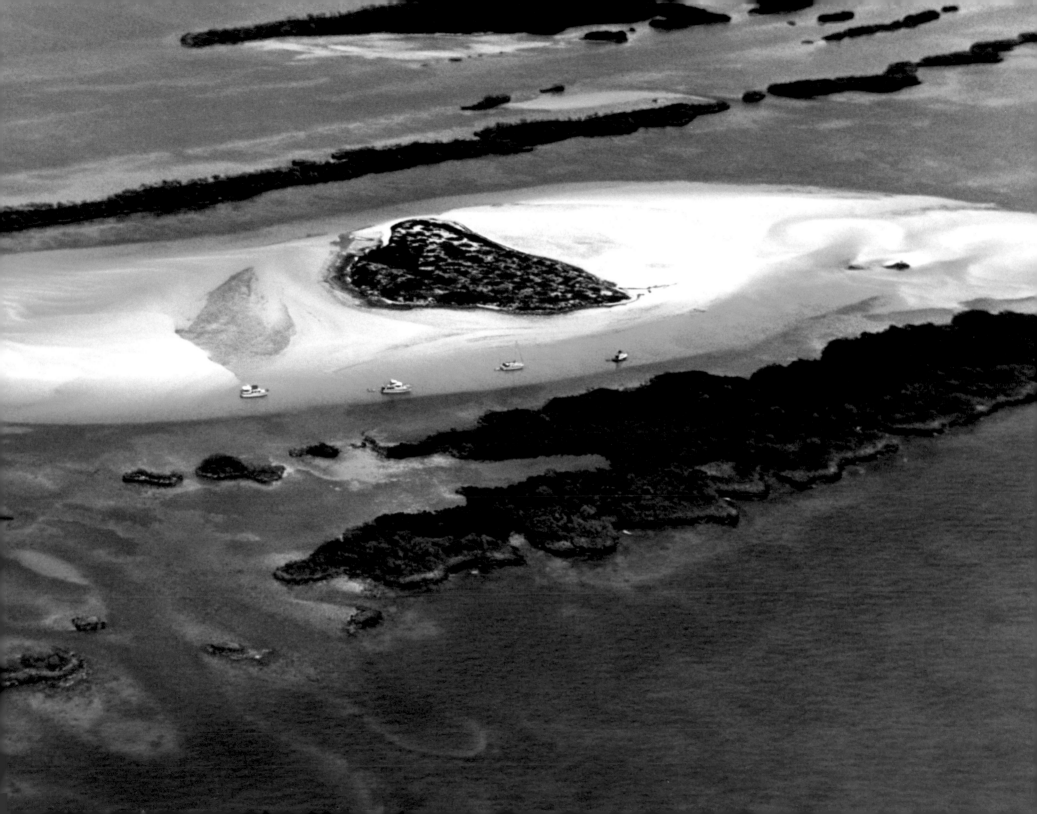

CARTER CAYS

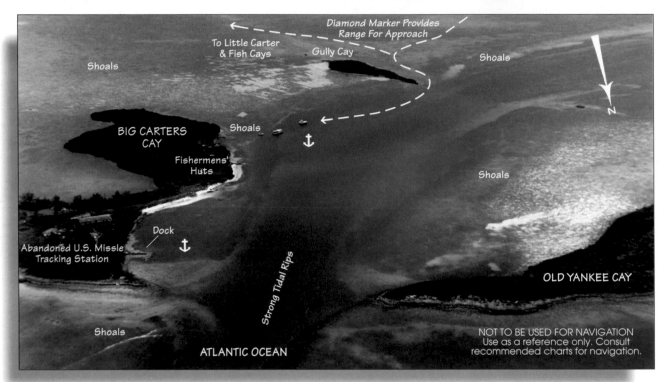

On map:
To Little Carter & Fish Cays
Diamond Marker Provides Range For Approach
Gully Cay
Shoals
Shoals
N
Shoals
BIG CARTERS CAY
Shoals
Fishermens' Huts
Shoals
Dock
Abandoned U.S. Missle Tracking Station
Strong Tidal Rips
OLD YANKEE CAY
Shoals
ATLANTIC OCEAN
NOT TO BE USED FOR NAVIGATION
Use as a reference only. Consult recommended charts for navigation.

The anchorage offers good protection in most wind conditions. However, keep in mind that strong tidal currents sweep through this anchorage. For this reason, it's not advisable to anchor in the deeper water of the harbour. This is where the current will be the strongest. Instead, move in closer to where the water begins to shoal.

ASHORE

The cays in this area are deserted, and you may often find you have this anchorage to yourself.

There are a few small sandy beaches ashore on Carter Cay littered with thousands of conch shells deposited by fishermen who sometimes live in the neighboring shacks. The fishermen seek both conch and crawfish.

The rocky shores of the surrounding islands provide exploration and snorkeling by dinghy, and bonefishing would appear exceptional on the many flats. For one thing, there is likely to be little or no fishing pressure.

The entrance to the Carter Cay anchorage can be somewhat tricky because of the numerous sandy shoals surrounding the area. The shoals are visible in favorable light conditions however, this is an area with continually shifting sand banks.

NAVIGATION

When approaching from the south, you must skirt a series of sandy shoals forming the Carter Cays Bank to the north.

There is a diamond-shaped range marker on Gully Cay to aid in your approach. As with many markers

or ranges in the Bahamas, you cannot always rely on their presence or accuracy. The towers of the abandoned U.S. missile base and its buildings, as well as a cluster of fishing shacks, are visible as you approach Gully Cay.

Approach the cay within about 50 feet, and then follow the shoreline into the harbour. Once inside, you will pass a small cay to port. Steer to the north between Gully Cay and Carter Cay where you will find good holding in 12-15 feet of water. Keep from straying towards the east or west where it shoals rapidly.

MORAINE CAY

To Allans - Pensacola Cay
To Fish Cays
N
Shoals
Beach
Excellent Snorkeling Over Reefs
Beach
Shoals
Reef
MORAINE CAY
Reef
Reef

NOT TO BE USED FOR NAVIGATION
Use as a reference only. Consult
recommended charts for navigation.

ASHORE

The main attractions of Moraine Cay are its beaches. One beach is located on the ocean side, and the other flanks the anchorage. Both are among the finest you will find among this area of Abaco.

The ocean beach can be reached by walking along the trails found on the cay. Moraine is privately owned, but uninhabited. Much of the island is in its natural state, which adds greatly to its appeal. Make certain that the beaches are left as litter-free as you found them.

The reefs surrounding this cay provide great opportunities for unforgettable snorkeling from the beach or a dinghy.

Surrounding flats provide good prospects for bonefishing and, likewise you could expect the reef fishing to be equally rewarding.

Considering all that it has to offer, Moraine Cay should be a stop on any cruiser's scheduled plans.

Picture yourself on a deserted South Seas island and it could be Moraine Cay. Surrounded by spectacular reefs and white sandy beaches, Moraine Cay provides an outstanding anchorage along its southern shore.

This naturally-formed harbour is fairly well protected from all wind directions except the south when it is fully exposed. It provides good holding in several feet of water and offers incredible views of the beach and nearby reefs.

NAVIGATION

The approach to the anchorage is straight-forward. On a northerly course head, directly towards the beach. Three small cays and reefs are visible to the east of the anchorage. Nearing the beach, you can anchor in 7-10 feet over a grassy bottom.

The anchorage is large enough to handle a number of boats with room to spare. It is possible to anchor as close to the beach as you are at ease with.

ALLANS - PENSACOLA CAY

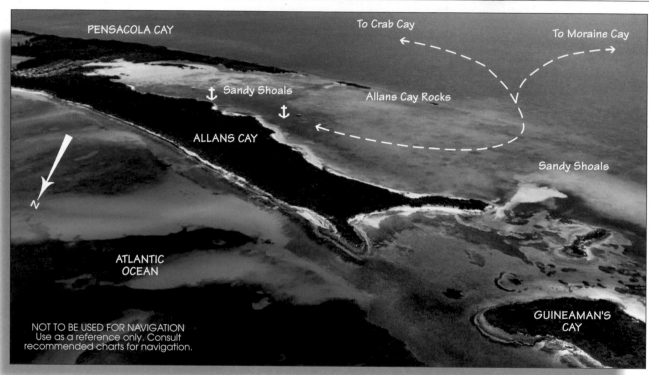

PENSACOLA CAY

To Crab Cay

To Moraine Cay

Sandy Shoals

Allans Cay Rocks

ALLANS CAY

Sandy Shoals

ATLANTIC
OCEAN

GUINEAMAN'S
CAY

N

NOT TO BE USED FOR NAVIGATION
Use as a reference only. Consult
recommended charts for navigation.

coral bottom in 6-8 feet of water.

At the eastern end of the cay is an interesting hurricane hole that could provide protection from winds out of all directions. Within this small harbour, you would be completely protected.

While the entrance to the hurricane hole is easily navigated, the drawback is the depth. It is under 3 feet MLW. Should you require the use of this harbour for any reason, the best plan would be to enter and exit at a high tide. Even then, you must be aware of your draft limitations.

ASHORE

Exploring the cay, you are likely to discover the ruins of the old government base. There were once several buildings and a helicopter pad on the island.

The best beaches will be found on the oceanside. Here, you will also find some reef for snorkeling.

The hurricane hole at the eastern tip of Allans - Pensacola Cay.

Allans - Pensacola Cay was once two separate cays. A storm had closed the bight between the two islands, and now they are referred to as one.

This was also once a U.S. government site, used as a missile tracking and communications station.

NAVIGATION

The anchorage harbour, located near the western section of the cay, is easily entered from the west or points to the south. The natural harbour provides good shelter from all winds except the northwest when it is fairly exposed.

Traveling from the southeast, you must round Allans Cay Rocks before entering the harbour. Navigation into the harbour and ease of access are among the reasons this anchorage is popular.

Once inside the harbour, favor the northern shoreline and stay to the west. The harbour shallows to 2 or 3 feet within its inner section. Reportedly, the harbour can be quite buggy in periods of calm weather and during the summer months.

The anchorage offers fair holding in a grassy and

SPANISH CAY MARINA

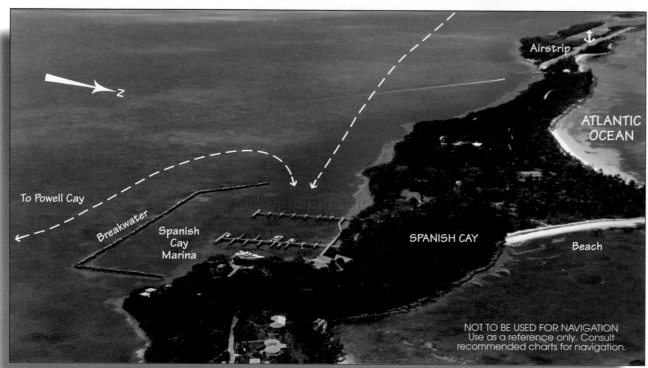

NOT TO BE USED FOR NAVIGATION
Use as a reference only. Consult
recommended charts for navigation.

O ver the years, the private island of Spanish Cay has been developed as a major resort complex and marina. While suffering damage from Hurricane Floyd, repairs were underway and largely completed within months after the major storm.

NAVIGATION

Spanish Cay is accessible from the ocean at either of the island's northern or southern tips. Reefs border the cay on its eastern shore. Two breaks are found at either end providing passage. They are not shown in these photos, so consult your charts and guides for instructions.

The entrance to the marina is found at the southern portion of the cay. An extensive breakwater encompasses much of the marina. A marked channel leads into the marina at the opening in the breakwater.

Inside is a modern marine facility with about 60 slips that can handle the largest of yachts. Surrounded by rocky bluffs, the setting is tropical and exotic. However, despite the breakwater, currents can be strong within the marina. Keep this in mind when docking or departing.

ASHORE

Spanish Cay is a fascinating island to explore with many walking paths scattered throughout the property. Golf carts are also available for rent.

The Inn at Spanish Cay offers luxury accommodations in either suites or apartments. A 5,000-foot airstrip is available for private or charter use.

The marina has all of the amenities found commonly with a resort-style facility.

Additionally, there is a restaurant, The Point House, and a bar, the Wreckers' Light, located adjacent to the marina.

An anchorage is located at the north end of the island in a harbour bordering the airstrip. From the south, you must round Squances Cay. The entrance is shoal with depths in the 4-foot range. Inside the anchorage, depths are in 8-9 feet with fair to poor holding. However, this anchorage is protected from all winds except the north. Enter the anchorage in only the most favorable light and sea conditions because of shoals at the entrance.

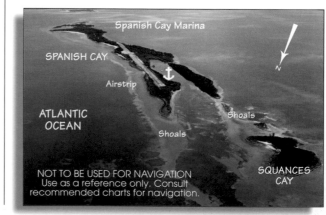

NOT TO BE USED FOR NAVIGATION
Use as a reference only. Consult
recommended charts for navigation.

COOPERS TOWN, GREAT ABACO

Coopers Town Shell

COOPERS TOWN,
GREAT ABACO ISLAND

NOT TO BE USED FOR NAVIGATION
Use as a reference only. Consult
recommended charts for navigation.

Note: Photo was taken prior
to Hurricane Flyod.

Hurricane Floyd heavily damaged Coopers Town. While this is one of the largest settlements in Abaco, it is situated on a totally exposed shore. Consequently, the damage from this major storm was substantial.

Reportedly, Coopers Town Shell, which has long been a favored fueling spot, was destroyed, and likewise the public dock. There was also fuel available at a dock for Murray's Service Station, but it is unknown how it fared during the storm. However, it is likely all will be reconstructed in the near future. It would be advisable to radio ahead before planning on fueling here.

NAVIGATION

There is no trick to approaching Coopers Town. The waters off the settlement are free of any hazards or obstructions. The telephone tower is a landmark. It is possible to drop your anchor just about anywhere off the settlement and dinghy into town. There are no marinas at this community.

Holding is good in 10-15 feet of water. However, keep in mind that this is an anchorage which is fully exposed from all wind directions except the west.

During unsettled weather, nearby Powell Cay may offer better protection, depending upon the wind direction. Powell provides popular anchorages and offers great beaches and exploration. Powell's popularity is partly due to its proximity to Coopers Town where supplies are available.

ASHORE

Coopers Town lacks the glamour that you may find in other tourist and resort- based communities. Nonetheless, it is an interesting community with friendly and accommodating residents.

While this is the largest settlement in northern Great Abaco, don't expect every convenience or service. The economy revolves largely around crawfish, conch and fishing.

There are a couple of grocery stores within walking distance from the shore. Additionally, you will find a few bakeries, liquor stores, a bar and a couple of restaurants.

Coopers Town as a destination remains most convenient for restocking your supplies while cruising northern Abaco.

Crawfish, conch and fish contribute heavily to the Coopers Town economy.

MANJACK & CRAB CAYS

MANJACK ROCKS

ATLANTIC OCEAN

Beach

N

MANJACK CAY

To Green Turtle

RAT CAY

NOT TO BE USED FOR NAVIGATION
Use as a reference only. Consult
recommended charts for navigation.

CRAB CAY

The most popular anchorage is the bight formed between Manjack and Crab Cays. The approach into the anchorage is straightforward, without any hazards of reefs or rocks. Anchor in the area adjacent to Rat Cay. Within the anchorage there is good holding in 8-10 feet over a grassy, sand bottom.

Most often there will be several other boats in this area, however, the anchorage is large enough to accommodate a small fleet. It is also exposed to winds from the west.

ASHORE

Manjack has forests of tall casuarinas pines that provide welcome shade for picnics. The pines flank a rocky shore that is perfect for hiking and beachcombing. It is a wild shoreline with countless interesting rock formations.

Snorkeling from the beach is outstanding. The rock and coral reef extends close inshore, and it teems with fish and other undersea life.

There is an inlet and harbour formed by the bight between Crab and Manjack, however, it is shallow. Depths are a foot or two at low tide. It is comprised of mangroves and grassy flats. Prospects for bonefishing should be excellent throughout this area.

There are also many areas around Manjack and Crab, ideal for dinghy exploration. There is a shallow passage between the north end of Green Turtle Cay and Fiddle Cay. Reef fishing from a small boat should be rewarding.

Manjack and Crab Cays offer a number of anchorage options, all of which provide stunning beaches and appealing seclusion.

Located just north of Green Turtle Cay, these anchorages are frequented by cruising boaters for picnics and overnight outings. The close proximity of New Plymouth for supplies is another plus if you are considering extended stays among these cays.

NAVIGATION

The northernmost anchorage is located at the tip of Manjack Cay and just off Manjack Channel. The wide channel provides easy access to the ocean.

Anchor in the pocket between Manjack and Manjack Rocks. While this is an attractive anchorage, it is exposed to the northwest and is subject to conditions that prevail in the ocean.

Another anchorage in the northern section of Manjack is located in a large bay just to the southwest of Manjack Rocks. It offers good holding and shelter from all winds, except the west.

GREEN TURTLE CAY

Crab Cay

Manjack Cay

Bluff Harbour

Coco Bay

To Treasure Cay & Whale Cay Passage

White Sound

Shallow

ATLANTIC OCEAN

N

Government Dock

New Plymouth

Long Bay

GREEN TURTLE CAY

Shoals

Black Sound

Shoals

Gillam Bay

NOT TO BE USED FOR NAVIGATION
Use as a reference only. Consult
recommended charts for navigation.

Shoals

ASHORE

Steeped in history, the New Plymouth settlement is one of the most picturesque in the Bahamas. The houses of the community are often compared to an early Cape Cod style. The settlement's links with history are displayed in the Albert Lowe Museum and the Memorial Sculpture Garden. The garden displays bronze busts of individuals who were important in the founding of the Bahamas and Abaco. The museum features a great deal of memorabilia dealing with the earliest days of Abaco. Both are worthwhile visits.

Choices in restaurants in New Plymouth are widely varied. Among them are the New Plymouth Inn, McIntosh Take-Away, Islands Restaurant and Grill, Laura's Kitchen, Rooster's Rest Pub, the Wrecking Tree and Mike's Bar N' Restaurant. The New Plymouth Inn also provides accommodations. Other cottages and rooms are available for rent.

Additionally, three grocery stores are located in New Plymouth. They include Lowe's, Curry's and Sid's. All provide a variety of products, and cater to supplying ship's stores for cruisers. Two hardware stores, Roberts Hardware and Marine and New Plymouth Hardware offer most goods, as well as some marine supplies. Gift shops include Loyalist Rose, Sand Dollar Shop, Shell Hut, Vert's Model Ship Shop and Ocean Blue Gallery.

A sculpture in the New Plymouth Memorial Sculpture Garden.

Neatly kept homes and shops reminiscent of a bygone era, narrow streets, flower gardens and friendly residents characterize the New Plymouth settlement on Green Turtle Cay. With a colorful history dating back to the founding of Abaco, this community is a popular port of call among all cruisers.

NAVIGATION

The favored fair-weather anchorage is located just off the northwestern shores of New Plymouth. It is an expansive area with fair to good holding in

8-10 feet of water. Keep in mind, this area can be uncomfortable for anchoring in unsettled weather, as it is exposed to the west and north. During heavy weather, it would be best to seek out better shelter in White or Black Sounds. Nonetheless, this anchorage area is popular because of the swinging room and convenience of reaching the settlement.

The neighboring settlement harbour with an entrance just off the Government Dock, is navigable by small boats and dinghies, but it is not recommended for anchoring.

BLUFF CAY HARBOUR & COCO BAY

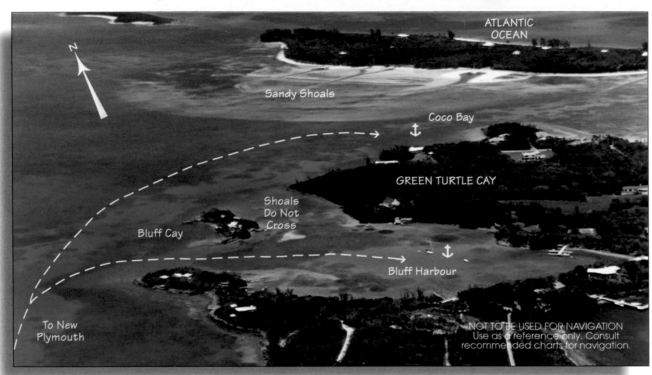

ATLANTIC OCEAN

Sandy Shoals

Coco Bay

GREEN TURTLE CAY

Shoals
Do Not
Cross

Bluff Cay

Bluff Harbour

To New
Plymouth

NOT TO BE USED FOR NAVIGATION
Use as a reference only. Consult
recommended charts for navigation.

northerly and westerly winds. In times of blustery weather with winds from those directions, it probably should not be considered or used as an overnight anchorage.

Nearby Bluff Harbour is much better protected. In fact, this is a beatifully formed natural harbour, offering shelter from all wind directions (except due north). The disadvantage of this anchorage is that there is no public landing on its shores since it is private property.

The harbour is entered by passing between the mainland of Green Turtle Cay and south of Bluff Cay Rock. Do not attempt to pass through on the north side of the rock since it is shoal. The passage into the harbour ranges from 4-5 feet in depth at MLW. Once inside, you can venture towards the western reaches of the harbour and anchor with fair holding in several feet of water. Respect the property owners' rights and do not venture to shore from the private docks.

Two attractive and protected anchorages are located at the northern section of Green Turtle Cay. The Bluff Harbour and Coco Bay anchorages are closely situated to each other, and often are largely unoccupied by other cruisers. Much of the property surrounding these anchorages is private and under development. Consequently, ashore activities are limited to exploration via dinghy to neighboring islands and beaches.

NAVIGATION

Coco Bay is tucked away at the northern tip of

Green Turtle Cay. The bay can be approached from the north by skirting the visible shoals and Crab Rock. From the south, you must round Bluff Harbour. While the bay shores boast beautiful, white sand beaches, the waters are shallow in this area. At low tide, it may even be difficult to reach the beach by dinghy without wading inshore. The water shoals to under 4 feet for much of the distance extending from the northernmost portion of Green Turtle Cay. However, Coco Bay is a pleasant anchorage, which you may often have to yourself. The anchorage is exposed to

ASHORE

If you feel the need to venture ashore, you can reach White Sound, Black Sound or the settlement harbour via a short dinghy ride.

There is also exceptional snorkeling, beachcombing and dinghy exploration just to the north of these anchorages at Manjack and Crab Cays.

WHITE SOUND, GREEN TURTLE CAY

Bluff Harbour

Coco Bay

Green Turtle Club

Bluff House Marina & Resort

White Sound

Dolphin Marine

Well Marked Channel

Shallow

Shoals

To Manjack & Crab Cays

N

To New Plymouth

GREEN TURTLE CAY

NOT TO BE USED FOR NAVIGATION
Use as a reference only. Consult
recommended charts for navigation.

White Sound at Green Turtle Cay provides an exceptional anchorage, as well as being home to two major Abaco resorts and marinas that cater to yachtsmen and fishermen. They are the Green Turtle Club and Bluff House.

NAVIGATION

The channel into White Sound is clearly marked and newly dredged carrying an average of 5-7 feet MLW. Stay within the immediate channel, since it shoals sharply outside on both sides. As you enter, you will pass Dolphin Marine on the port side.

They provide boat sales, as well as being an OMC distributor and dealer for Evinruide and Johnson. Repairs and a wide selection of parts are available.

Once inside the sound, you'll enter a large anchorage area with depths ranging from 8-10 feet. Holding is good in a grassy bottom.

To starboard, you will see the entrance to another large bay. However, do not venture into this area with anything other than an outboard vessel. The depths are shallow, and it is best visited only for bonefishing.

White Sound is well protected in all directions

from winds, although, the surrounding area did sustain substantial damage during Floyd.

ASHORE

A considerable amount of expansion and remodeling has been going on at Bluff House, which is found on the western shore of the sound. This resort features a marina with fuel service, accommodations, a beatifully appointed dining room and a spectacular view from the bluff-top pool. Overlooking the Sea of Abaco, the views from this resort are unparalleled, particularly at sunset.

Across White Sound is the Green Turtle Club. It also features a full-service marina, rooms and villas, lounges and an attractive dining room with evening dinner specials. Green Turtle Club is host to a major fishing tournament held each summer.

Both resorts are among the most popular in Abaco, and each has a boutique. Because of their popularity, it is best to call ahead for both dockage and dinner reservations. While it is quite a hike into New Plymouth, alternatively, the resorts will provide transportation to the settlement. There are fine beaches on the oceanside.

The sound is also home to Brendal's Dive Center. Having been established on Green Turtle for many years, Brendal's provides dive and snorkel trips, scuba instruction, kayak rentals and special boat charters.

BLACK SOUND, GREEN TURTLE CAY

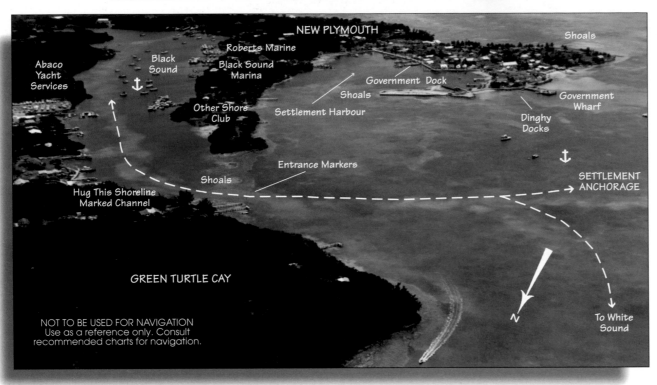

NEW PLYMOUTH

Roberts Marine

Black Sound

Black Sound Marina

Abaco Yacht Services

Government Dock

Shoals

Shoals

Other Shore Club

Settlement Harbour

Government Wharf

Dinghy Docks

Entrance Markers

SETTLEMENT ANCHORAGE

Hug This Shoreline Marked Channel

Shoals

GREEN TURTLE CAY

To White Sound

NOT TO BE USED FOR NAVIGATION
Use as a reference only. Consult
recommended charts for navigation.

Black Sound is a popular and protected anchorage for cruisers visiting Green Turtle Cay. A major attraction of the anchorage is that New Plymouth is just a short walk or dinghy ride away. Additionally, there are marinas that offer dockage and moorings.

NAVIGATION

The entrance to Black Sound is just to the northwest of Settlement Harbour. A spit of land extends to the north. This point must be rounded, leading into a narrow, but well-marked channel.

Entering the channel can be a bit intimidating the first time, especially in a deeper draft vessel. However, if you stay within the channel, you'll find depths of approximately 3-5 feet MLW. If your vessel draws more, you may have to wait for high tide to enter or depart.

Once inside there is a fairly roomy anchorage with good holding in a grassy bottom with depths in the 10-foot range.

ASHORE

As you enter the sound, to port you will pass one of the best boatyards in Abaco. Abaco Yacht Services has long been recognized for fine services and fair prices. The company has a large travel-lift and provides a wide range of services including bottom painting and storage. If you are looking for storage, make reservations well ahead, especially during hurricane season.

Dockage, fuel, showers, water, ice and limited accommodations are available at the Other Shore Club. This marina is located starboard immediately after entering the sound.

Further into the sound, you will find the Black Sound Marina, also to starboard. This marina also offers dockage, water, showers and ice, but not fuel. It is situated in a attractive setting and a short walk into New Plymouth.

Another business that should be noted within Black Sound, is Roberts Marine. This location is actually the workshop for Roberts Marine and Roberts Hardware, located near the town dock in New Plymouth. At the Black Sound location, outboard service is available, as well as sales and parts for Evinrude and Johnson. They also provide diesel services.

Rush hour in downtown New Plymouth. by Kathy Find

NO NAME CAY

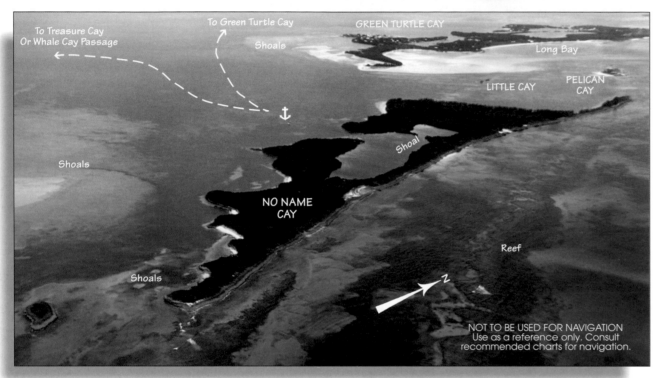

To Treasure Cay
Or Whale Cay Passage

To Green Turtle Cay

GREEN TURTLE CAY

Shoals

Long Bay

LITTLE CAY

PELICAN
CAY

Shoals

Shoal

NO NAME
CAY

Reef

Shoals

N

NOT TO BE USED FOR NAVIGATION
Use as a reference only. Consult
recommended charts for navigation.

Lying just to the south of Green Turtle Cay and north of Whale Cay, is uninhabited No Name Cay. The anchorage at this cay is considered best for daytime use only. It is completely exposed from the southwest and west. Likewise, rough conditions in the ocean are likely to influence the anchorage waters.

NAVIGATION

Traveling from Green Turtle Cay, in order to reach this anchorage, you must skirt the expansive sand bank that extends to the southwest between the two cays. Depths on these shoals are only a couple of feet. However, in decent light, you can visually navigate along the edge of the bank where you will find water averaging about 10 feet.

From the south, after making a Whale Cay passage, there are also shoals that must be avoided to the west of No Name. These are also easy to spot. Once you have passed the shoals, you can take up a heading towards the cay.

The anchorage is located just off the entrance of a lagoon on the western shore about midway along the cay. Here there is fair holding and

protection from winds out of the east and northeast.

The lagoon can only be entered by dinghy at mid or high tide. A rocky bar extends across the entrance. Once inside, the best depths will be found at the southern section. It is shallow to the north. Lined with mangroves, the lagoon provides interesting exploration by dinghy.

ASHORE

There is a small beach to the north of the lagoon entrance where you can beach your dinghy for a swim. The cay's shores are largely only accessible by dinghy.

The best beaches are to the northwest of the No Name anchorage at Pelican Cay. While Pelican can be reached with a boat drawing 3 feet or more, it also is surrounded by shifting sand banks. It may be best to anchor at No Name and then travel by dinghy. Bear in mind this should only be attempted in fair and calm weather. Pelican Cay and the surrounding smaller cays are exposed to the ocean.

Besides the outstanding beaches on Pelican Cay, there is also good snorkeling and diving on the surrounding reef.

Big Channel to the north of Pelican Cay leads to the ocean where you can explore more reefs in deeper waters.

There are good fishing prospects in this area, both on the reef and while trolling the edges of the reef.

WHALE CAY

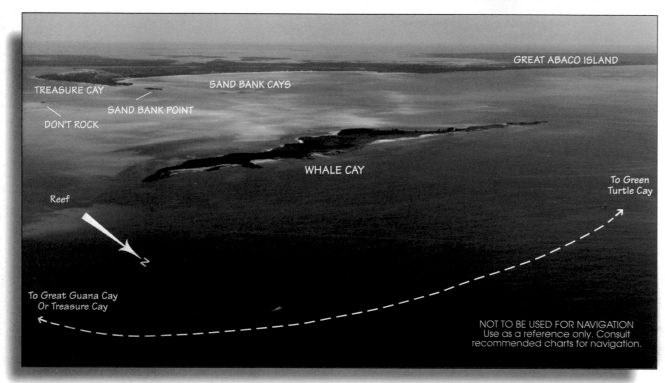

Labels on image: GREAT ABACO ISLAND · SAND BANK CAYS · TREASURE CAY · SAND BANK POINT · DON'T ROCK · WHALE CAY · Reef · To Green Turtle Cay · To Great Guana Cay Or Treasure Cay

NOT TO BE USED FOR NAVIGATION
Use as a reference only. Consult
recommended charts for navigation.

Whale Cay impassable are "rages". A rage occurs when offshore disturbances create high seas and swells that sweep ashore making venturing out of any Abaco pass extremely dangerous.

The scope of these photos does not include all the references necessary for a safe Whale Cay passage. It is meant as a pictorial only, and it is suggested that you consult your charts and guides carefully. Some of the best directions are found in Steve Dodge's *The Cruising Guide To Abaco Bahamas*.

Even more important, before setting out around Whale Cay, is determining whether this passage can be made safely. It is advisable to listen to all available reports on the conditions at Whale Cay before venturing into the ocean. One of the best sources is the daily cruiser's net broadcast on VHF 68 at 8:15 am. If possible, contact other vessels making the passage, or reach someone anchored in Baker's Bay who may be able to report on conditions.

Baker's Bay is the logical holding pattern anchorage for those traveling north. Located at the northern tip of Great Guana Cay, this anchorage is the best stepping-off point, especially if it is necessary to wait for safe conditions to make the passage. Here, you are also bound to be in the company of other boats faced with the same decision.

Regardless of the weather conditions, always make certain everything and everyone are secured when rounding Whale Cay. Even in calm weather you can encounter swells that make the passage uncomfortable.

Preparing for the passage around Whale Cay is likely to include some anxiety on part of the captain and crew, and it is justifiable. The Whale Cay passage is commonly recognized as potentially the most dangerous navigation a cruiser will encounter in Abaco.

Large ocean going freighters have been known to capsize with loss of lives attempting this passage. The possible hazards of rounding Whale Cay should be taken seriously, especially in any rough weather.

NAVIGATION

The sand bank that extends from Whale Cay, across the Sea of Abaco to Treasure Cay, makes the ocean passage around Whale Cay a necessity for nearly all boats. The inshore routes are recommended for shoal draft vessels. Local knowledge is suggested.

The accompanying photos depict the sort of conditions for the passage that everyone hopes for. This may be common during summer months, but more of a rarity during much more windy periods. Another consideration which makes

BAKER'S BAY, GREAT GUANA CAY

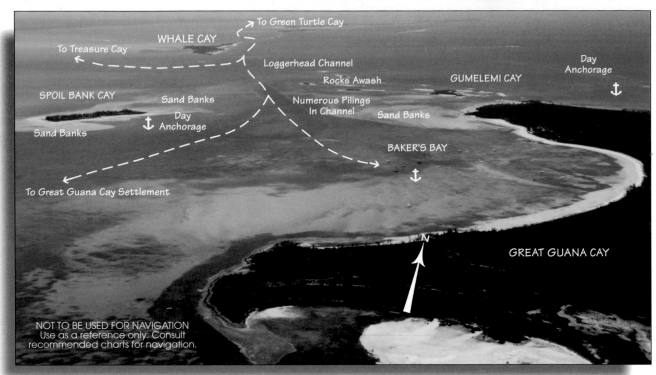

To Green Turtle Cay
WHALE CAY
To Treasure Cay
Loggerhead Channel
Rocks Awash
GUMELEMI CAY
Day Anchorage
SPOIL BANK CAY
Sand Banks
Numerous Pilings In Channel
Day Anchorage
Sand Banks
Sand Banks
BAKER'S BAY
To Great Guana Cay Settlement
N
GREAT GUANA CAY

NOT TO BE USED FOR NAVIGATION
Use as a reference only. Consult
recommended charts for navigation.

As the favorite steeping off point for rounding Whale Cay heading north, Baker's Bay was once utilized by a cruise ship line as a stop-over destination. In the early 90's the Premier Cruise Line decided the passage through Loggerhead Channel was entirely too rough at times and abandoned Baker's Bay as an anchorage.

NAVIGATION

Located at the northern tip of Great Guana Cay, spacious Baker's Bay is frequented by cruisers who are either preparing to set out around Whale Cay to points north, or for those who have made the passage. Generally, it is a good spot to sit and wait out any unfavorable weather. You will usually find yourself in the company of several other boats with the same plans.

The bay is located to the east of the ship's channel dredged by the cruise line. Numerous markers remain which were utilized by the cruise ship. There is also a turning basin just off the bay.

Entering Baker's Bay is simply a matter of heading east towards the shoreline and anchoring in several feet of water. Holding is fair over a grass and sand bottom. The bay is exposed to winds from the west and south, however, it does provide fair shelter from northers. There are docks on the beach, but the property remains private.

Nearby Spoil Bank Cay, just to the west, also offers anchorage possibilities. However, this should only be considered in fair weather. It is subject to swells rolling in from the ocean.

ASHORE

Baker's Bay has a sweeping semicircular beach that is exceptionally scenic. This was one of the major attractions offered by the cruise line. Beaches also totally encircle Spoil Bank Cay which was created when the shipping channel was dredged. The shelling on this spoil bank is excellent.

Another notable beach is located at the northern tip of Great Guana Cay, just to the north of Baker's Bay. It is also possible to anchor here, but it is best reserved for fair weather only and not for overnighting. It is reached by passing between the tip of Guana and Gumelemi Cay. The area is surrounded by reef and rocks, is exposed to the ocean and should only be visited in calm conditions.

Besides the terrific beaches found in this area, there is also outstanding snorkeling along the reefs found at the northern tip of Great Guana Cay. The reefs abound with fish life, and the coral formations are notable.

SETTLEMENT HARBOUR, GREAT GUANA CAY

Labels on map: To Baker's Bay Whale Cay · DELIA'S CAY · Shoals, Do Not Cross · Guana Beach Resort & Marina · Flashing Light · Breakwater · Orchid Bay Marina · Settlement Harbour · Public Dockage · To Coco Beach Resort · Nipper's · GREAT GUANA CAY · NOT TO BE USED FOR NAVIGATION Use as a reference only. Consult recommended charts for navigation.

Great Guana Cay boasts some of the most beautiful beaches in the Bahamas. It is also one of the longest islands in the Abaco chain, stretching more than five miles with pristine beaches on both shores.

The settlement is found in a picturesque harbour that is easily entered, and provides fair holding in a grassy, sand bottom. During peak cruising periods, you are likely to find the marinas filled to capacity and the anchorage often crowded.

Enter the harbour by passing between the breakwater and the point of land just to the west.

Depths in the anchorage range from 5-10 feet. The harbour can become uncomfortable in strong blows from the southwest.

Many cruisers opt for the swinging room and excellent holding offered by the nearby Delia's Cay anchorage. While exposed from the southwest, this area is the logical alternative when the settlement harbour is too crowded for comfortable anchoring. A brief dinghy trip puts you ashore at the settlement.

Orchid Bay Yacht Club & Marina is the newest development in the settlement. The full-service marina can accommodate 64 vessels, and provides Texaco fuel. A pool and restaurant are planned. Orchid Bay is the site of a substantial development offering exclusive beachfront and bayside homesites.

Dockage and fuel is also available at the Guana Beach Resort & Marina. A fire destroyed the restaurant facilities at the resort, however, contruction was underway to rebuild at press time.

Popular spots ashore include Nipper's Beach Bar & Grill and Coco Bay Club, both with restaurants and bars overlooking the ocean. Both facilities cater to cruisers.

Nipper's, which holds Sunday pig roasts, provides free golf cart transportation for visitors. Coco Bay is a short walk from the dinghy docks. Snorkeling and beachcombing is exceptional along the shoreline. On the bayside, the Dolphin Beach Resort provides accommodations and a restaurant.

Ashore there is plenty of dinghy dockage, a post office, Batelco phone office, grocery, hardware and a liquor store. There are also several other shops. The settlement is a neat and orderly community currently undergoing a transition being brought on by development, and new homes are being built throughout the island.

A colorful vessel at Great Guana Cay. by Kathy Find

TREASURE CAY, GREAT ABACO

Marked Channel

Sand Banks

Tower (Helps Locate Channel Entrance)

Fuel Dock

Golf Course

TREASURE CAY

Anchorage & Moorings

Marina

N

ASHORE

As the centerpiece of a large vacation complex, Treasure Cay Hotel Resort, the marina boasts all of the amenities you would commonly find at the finer marine facilities stateside. This includes a golf course, marina rooms and villas, the Tipsy Seagull Bar, the Spinnaker Restaurant, swimming pools, laundry, cable television, marine store, grocery and other shops. Fishing charters and boat rentals are available. A dive shop is on the premises with dive trips and instruction available. The marina is also host to a major Bahamas fishing tournament, the Treasure Cay International Billfish Tournament, which has been staged early each summer for nearly two decades.

Treasure Cay offers a beach that is regarded as one of the finest in the world. Stretching for about three miles in a semicircular shoreline, this beach is outstanding for walking, sunbathing, swimming and other watersports. A beach bar and restaurant are part of the resort complex.

The marina and resort are located a short drive from the Treasure Cay Airport, where flights are regularly available stateside by several carriers.

Treasure Cay Beach

The Treasure Cay Marina has long been recognized as one of the premiere yachting and sport-fishing facilities of the Abaco islands. The marina, is also among the largest in Abaco with 150 slips in a well-protected harbour. While Hurricane Floyd wreaked havoc among other parts of Abaco, the marina sustained little damage.

NAVIGATION

Sandy shoals flank the channel into the marina, but it is well-marked and easily negotiated, even for vessels in the 70-foot plus class. Depths in the channel are in the 6-foot range MLW. A lighted sign is found just off the entrance. Upon entering the channel, it curves to starboard, and then straight into the marina. The fuel dock is found on the port side as you enter. Then you will pass a mooring and anchoring harbour as you near the marina. Moorings are available for a fee at the marina office.

Boats approaching from northern destinations must round Whale Cay in order to reach Treasure Cay.

MAN-O-WAR CAY

ENTER AT APPROXIMATELY
26° 35.15 / 77° 00.16

DICKIE'S CAY

North Man-O-War Channel

Rocks

Settlement

MAN-O-WAR CAY

N

NOT TO BE USED FOR NAVIGATION
Use as a reference only. Consult
recommended charts for navigation.

The highly industrious and deeply religious residents, which comprise the community on Man-O-War Cay, make this island one of the most unique in Abaco. With a fascinating history dating back to the founding of Abaco, Man-O-War has long been linked with boat building.

Today, the craftsmen of the island are still recognized as some of the finest in ship carpentry. In fact, it is not uncommon to spot many stateside boats in the local boatyards that have traveled specifically to this island in order to take advantage of the workmanship available.

NAVIGATION

The entrance to the two separate Man-O-War harbours is well marked, but extremely narrow. For this reason, it's advisable to avoid meeting other vessels when entering or departing. It is best to enter the harbour slightly to the south. This should put you directly in the channel and allow you to sight other departing craft.

Once inside, you have your choice of veering off to the starboard channel into the Eastern Harbour, or turning to port towards the main settlement harbour. Pay close attention to the markers, but also read the deepest depths of the channel visually.

Usually, you will find the Eastern Harbour less crowded for anchoring. However, during peak cruising periods, expect both to be packed tightly.

ASHORE

The Man-O-War Marina, which provides dockage, fuel and water, is located to starboard in the main harbour. It is always recommended to call ahead for reservations. The Pavillion Restaurant, adjacent to the marina, serves lunch and dinner. A dive shop and gift shop are also on the marina grounds.

Two boatyards are located in the harbour: Edwin's Boat Yard #1 and #2. These yards offer a wide variety of supplies, and provide service and repairs. Other supplies are found at Man-O-War Hardware and Building Supply.

Within the settlement there are two grocery stores, Albury's Harbour Grocery and the Man-O-War Grocery. Liquor, beer or wine are not sold on the island

Handcrafted canvas products such as bags, briefcases and hats are available at The Sail Shop. Joe's Studio features woodcraft, ceramics and books. Island Treasures and Belle Ena are also gift shops on the island.

Restaurants ashore include the Hibiscus Cafe and Ena's Place.

During a walking tour through this neat and orderly community, be sure to visit the oceanside beaches.

MARSH HARBOUR, GREAT ABACO

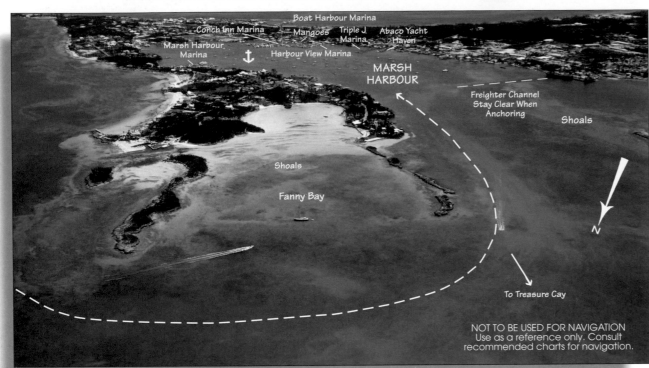

Boat Harbour Marina
Conch Inn Marina
Mangoes   Triple J   Abaco Yacht
Marsh Harbour   Marina   Haven
Marina   Harbour View Marina

MARSH
HARBOUR

Freighter Channel
Stay Clear When
Anchoring

Shoals

Shoals

Fanny Bay

N

To Treasure Cay

NOT TO BE USED FOR NAVIGATION
Use as a reference only. Consult
recommended charts for navigation.

Marsh Harbour may lack the scenery and charm which characterize many neighboring islands, but this bustling community makes up for it with a wealth of fine restaurants, excellent marine facilities, grocery stores and shopping. Likewise, whether you require electronics, engine, electrical, refrigeration or air conditioning repairs, you can count on fair and reliable assistance from local shops and marine suppliers.

NAVIGATION

Entrance into the harbour is simple once you locate the outer and inner point markers on the two small islands to the north of the main harbour. There are no hazards entering the harbour, although you may find floating buoys marking the shipping channel as you proceed. Follow the northern shore around into the expansive harbour. There, you will have good protection from winds from all directions and good holding in 6-10 feet of water. At times, the harbour can be quite crowded, but you should have little problem finding a spot with adequate swinging room.

One area to avoid while anchoring, is the ships' channel that also leads to the customs dock. The channel is to the northwest of the main harbour, and marked. There is considerable shipping traffic to these docks both day and night. Also, because of boats traveling about at all hours of the night and early morning, it's advisable to always have your anchor light on, and even a cabin light, to clearly identify your boat.

ASHORE

As an option to anchoring, you can select from several marinas including the Conch Inn, the Marsh Harbour Marina, Abaco Yacht Haven, Harbour View Marina, Mangoes and Triple J. Marina. All offer affordable dockage although it is best to call ahead for reservations. Some of these feature on site restaurants and lounges. Others are within walking distance to dining spots and grocery stores.

Regardless the day of the week, you can always count on something going on in Marsh Harbour. Restaurants and lounges, such as Sapodilly's Bar and Grill, the Conch Inn (also the Abaco home for The Moorings), Wally's, and the Jib Room at the Marsh Harbour Marina, have dining and entertainment specials geared to the cruising boater.

From Marsh Harbour, the daily "cruiser's net" is broadcast each morning at 8:15 on VHF Channel 68. Besides important weather information, the net provides visitors with a synopsis of everything going on in central Abaco.

BOAT HARBOUR MARINA, MARSH HARBOUR

Harbour View Marina

Mangoes

Conch Inn Marina

Marsh Harbour Marina

MARSH HARBOUR

ABACO BEACH RESORT & BOAT HARBOUR MARINA

Lighted Marker

Breakwater

To Sugarloaf Creek

NOT TO BE USED FOR NAVIGATION
Use as a reference only. Consult recommended charts for navigation.

Hurricane Floyd dealt the Abaco Beach Resort and Boat Harbour Marina a heavy blow. However, within months the marina was again operational and repairs to the resort completed.

This is one of the largest and most modern marinas in Abaco and a favorite among the mega-yachts which cruise the islands. It can accommodate yachts up to 200 feet.

NAVIGATION

Located on the southwest shore of Marsh Harbour, the Boat Harbour Marina is reached from

the north by rounding Point Set Rock and Matt Lowe's Cay. There is an area of shoals as you approach the marina, however, they are marked and should be visible in good light. A breakwater extends a fair distance from the shoreline, providing shelter within the marina. The entrance is located at the far eastern tip of the breakwater, and is also marked. The resort hotel and other buildings will be visible from a good distance off, and the approach is not difficult.

Boat Harbour Marina can also be reached by smaller craft with a shallow draft by passing

through Sugarloaf Creek. This passage extends along the eastern shore of the peninsula which makes up Marsh Harbour. This was once a favored anchorage area, but development and boat traffic has discouraged any anchoring. Should you travel through Sugarloaf Creek, do it at idle speed as there are many boat tied to docks along the creek.

ASHORE

Boat Harbour Marina has every convenience and amenity you could hope for. On the grounds there is the Angler's restaurant, a lounge, swimming pools, tennis courts, a boutique, liquor store and a grocery store. The beautifully maintained grounds of the resort are adjacent to the marina.

Abaco Beach Resort offers beachfront rooms and cottages. There is a dive operation at the resort, and all aspects of watersports. The marina is the Abaco base for Florida Yacht Charters (Bahamas) Ltd.

The marina and resort are also extremely popular among the sportfishing set. Four major fishing tournaments are staged from the marina each year.

While situated beyond the hustle and bustle of downtown Marsh Harbour, the marina is a short walk to the many shops and stores found in town.

Boat Harbour Marina at the Abaco Beach Resort.

MATT LOWE'S CAY

MARSH HARBOUR

SUGAR LOAF CAY

Boat Harbour Marina

Sugar Loaf Creek

To Point Set Rock

Shoals -- Small Boat Passage

MATT LOWE'S CAY

Day Anchorage

NOT TO BE USED FOR NAVIGATION
Use as a reference only. Consult
recommended charts for navigation.

N

Located a short distance from Marsh Harbour, Matt Lowe's Cay offers a pleasant anchorage that is protected except in strong westerlies.

As an alternative to the many boats you will find anchored in Marsh Harbour, this anchorage is often deserted, although there is plenty of room.

NAVIGATION

Matt Lowe's is a private island and the home ashore was damaged extensively by Hurricane Floyd. If you are lucky enough to have deep pockets, the cay is also for sale. The anchorage is located on the western shore, just beyond Sugar Loaf Creek. From Marsh Harbour, it is easily reached and the only feature which should be noted, is Sanka Shoal. However, this is marked with a stake and easily spotted. From the south or east, you must round Point Set Rock which is found just off the northern tip of Matt Lowe's Cay.

The anchorage is located in a horseshoe shaped bay with depths of 7-10 feet and fair holding over a grassy bottom. This anchorage offers good protection from strong winds out of the north and the east.

There are a series of small cays just south of the anchorage making up part of the Sugar Loaf Cay chain. It is possible to cross between Matt Lowe's Cay and these small cays. However, this should be attempted only in a small boat, and then in good light. There are coral heads and rocks through this pass that could cause propeller or lower unit damage.

ASHORE

Since Matt Lowe's Cay is a private island, privacy should be respected. In addition, the waters from the anchorage to the beach are extremely shallow.

However, there is good snorkeling and dinghy exploration around the Sugar Loaf Cays. Also, a short dinghy ride along Sugar Loaf Creek will lead you to Abaco Beach Resort and Boat Harbour Marina. There are grocery and liquor stores at the marina, as well as ice, should you need supplies.

Another point of interest in the vicinity is Mermaid Reef. This popular reef for snorkeling and diving is located to the east of the entrance to Marsh Harbour, just offshore. There are buoys marking the reef. These are day moorings for small boats. Fishing and spearfishing is prohibited over this reef.

If you are anchored or tied to a dock in Marsh Harbour, the anchorage at Matt Lowe's Cay offers a relaxing break away from the crowds for either a day outing or overnighting.

HOPE TOWN, ELBOW CAY

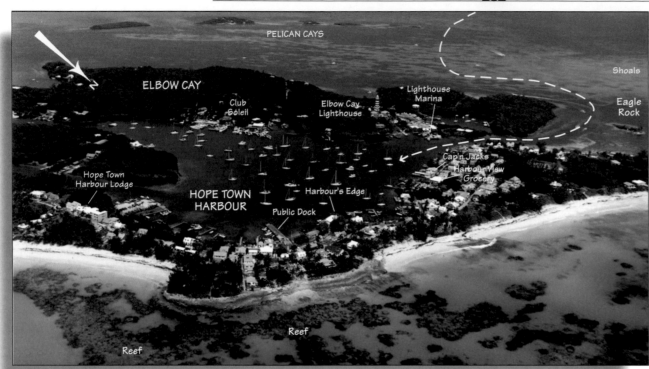

The Hope Town Lighthouse is often referred to as the most photographed site in the Bahamas. The lighthouse and the neighboring harbour deserve the distinction. Nowhere else in the islands of the Bahamas, are you likely to discover a more idyllic setting.

While the red and white striped lighthouse is the focal point of the harbour, Hope Town is also one of the most impressive ports of call in Abaco.

NAVIGATION

The entrance to Hope Town Harbour is easily navigated. Pass by North Parrot Cay, keeping it to starboard. On a southeast heading, spot the famous lighthouse and head towards shore, keeping it about 100 yards off. Take up a northerly heading along the shoreline until you spot Eagle Rock. There is a yellow home on the island. At that point, you will be able to pick up the channel markers, as well as range markers. Maintain idle speed through the channel and into the harbour.

Once inside, there is an expansive anchoring and mooring area, although, often the quarters are tight and moorings taken. Reservations for moorings are suggested. Almost always, you will find this harbour crowded.

If space is too tight for your liking, anchor outside the harbour to the east of Parrot Cays and dinghy ashore. You will find plenty of room in this anchorage area.

ASHORE

Inside the harbour, there are two marinas; Lighthouse Marina and Cottages and Hope Town Marina. The Lighthouse Marina offers fuel, a ship's store and repairs.

There are several good restaurants ashore. They include Club Soleil, Hope Town Harbour Lodge (which features an oceanfront pool and bar), Harbour's Edge and Captain Jack's.

For stocking up on supplies, there are two grocery stores; Vernon's and Harbour View, which provides a dinghy dock. For other needs, there is Village Hardware and Lighthouse Liquors.

Bicycles and golf carts are available for rent, and there is regularly scheduled pickups for garbage at the public dock.

Hope Town is the base for Abaco Bahamas Yacht Charters and Sail Abaco.

Gift shops include Ebb Tide, Edith's Straw Shop, Fantasy Boutique, Island Gallery, Kemps and El Mercado.

The Hope Town Yacht Club is also active with many fun-styled races throughout the year.

WHITE SOUND, ELBOW CAY

ATLANTIC OCEAN

The ocean swept over this area during Hurricane Floyd.

Abaco Inn

Sea Spray Marina

Shoals

Shoals

Well-Marked Channel

Shoals

WHITE SOUND

Shoals

ELBOW CAY

Shoals

Shoals

N

NOT TO BE USED FOR NAVIGATION
Use as a reference only. Consult recommended charts for navigation.

The White Sound area of Elbow Cay sustained some of the heaviest damage in the Hub of Abaco during Hurricane Floyd. Several houses in the sound were destroyed when Atlantic waters swept across this portion of the island.

However, repairs to the damage were quickly made, and what remains as testimony to the storm's strength are huge sand dunes seen at the top in the adjoining photos.

NAVIGATION

The entrance to White Sound, located about two miles south of Hope Town, is marked with a buoy which is lighted at night with a red flasher. Heading towards the east, two range markers will be visible at the Abaco Inn. This is a straightline course to the Inn. While there are no markers for the entrance channel, it is clearly visible with sand flats flanking both sides. The depth is approximately 5-6 feet MLW.

Before reaching the Inn, a marked channel will lead to the Sea Spray Resort Villas and Marina. The Sea Spray channel is about a 90-degree turn to the south. Just before reaching the marina, you will pass a rock breakwater to port.

ASHORE

White Sound is home to two favorite cruising destinations, the Abaco Inn and Sea Spray Resort Villas and Marina.

The Abaco Inn is a secluded, relaxing spot that provides 15 rooms directly on the ocean. Excellent dining is available on the Inn's outdoor patio, or inside dining room. They are open for lunch and dinner. Located about two miles from Hope Town, cruising boaters moored or anchored in the main harbour can arrange for transportation for dining by contacting the Inn. The Inn has a small marina for guests and visitors on the Sea of Abaco side. Call ahead on the VHF to determine whether slips are available. The Inn also features an oceanside pool and bar, as well as a gift shop and a lively cocktail lounge.

The Sea Spray Resort Villas and Marina is located in the southern reaches of the sound. The full-service marina provides deep-water access through a well-marked channel. The marina is well-protected and features a freshwater pool and the Garbonzo Bar, the Boat House Restaurant (open for breakfast, lunch and dinner), and boat rentals. Villas with ocean and harbour views are available. The resort complex and marina is located a short walk from the ocean beaches, and just over a three mile ride ashore to Hope Town. Complimentary transportation is provided for resort and marina guests.

TILLOO CUT

ATLANTIC OCEAN

White Sound

ELBOW CAY

Tahiti Beach

Shoals

TILLOO CUT

Rocks

Tilloo Cut Entrance
At Approximately
26° 29.89 / 76° 58.54

N

Rock

TILLOO CAY

To Lubber's Quarters Cay

Shoals

NOT TO BE USED FOR NAVIGATION
Use as a reference only. Consult
recommended charts for navigation.

Passing through the cut, there are a number of large homes on the southern tip of Elbow Cay. Tilloo Cut is the most convenient way to reach the ocean if you are docked at the Sea Spray Marina in White Sound.

ASHORE

While Tilloo Cut itself is of no interest as far as shoreside activities or sights, the surrounding area has many.

A popular anchorage is situated just to the north of the cut called Tahiti Beach. The beach has been justly named because of the tall palms along its shore. Many boaters anchor in the harbour adjacent to the beach and then dinghy in, enjoying swimming in crystal clear waters. The beach is exceptional.

The cut is additionally just east of a large island, Lubbers Quarters. Two restaurants are located on the island, Yahoes Sand Bar and Cracker P's. Both offer dockage, however, the depths are shallow, and it would be best to dinghy in. The restaurants offer very good food.

Lubbers Quarters is the home to the legendary Yahoe, a mythical bird-like creature with the toes of its feet mounted backwards, and seldom seen.

Tilloo Cut is known for very productive fishing. Because of the depths in the channel approaching the cut (often 30 feet plus) and the currents, there is an abundance of large table fish. You can expect action from snapper, grouper and a wide range of other species.

The colorful waters the Bahamas are famous for, are always on display in the vicinity of Tilloo Cut. Tilloo Cut is the ocean passage between Elbow Cay to the north and Tilloo Cay to the south.

As with all channels and passages in Abaco into the Atlantic, treat them with a good deal of respect. Heavy winds or rage conditions can make them impassable and potentially dangerous.

NAVIGATION

Depths throughout the channel leading into the ocean average 7-10 feet. Once you have cleared the cut, the water drops off sharply. A private island with a home is located just to the south of the cut. Round this island to the port, avoiding the shoals you will be able to spot to the south.

Keep the rock in the channel to starboard, staying towards the shoreline of Tilloo Cay. Exposed rocks are visible, and depths will drop as you approach the cut.

It is a simple passage to navigate into the ocean, without any markers. However, in good light conditions, you should be able to spot any shoals or rocks without any trouble.

SANDY CAY

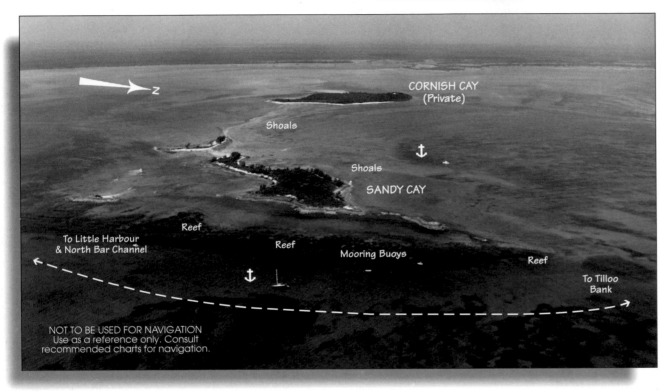

CORNISH CAY
(Private)

Shoals

Shoals

SANDY CAY

Reef

To Little Harbour
& North Bar Channel

Reef

Reef

Mooring Buoys

Reef

To Tilloo
Bank

NOT TO BE USED FOR NAVIGATION
Use as a reference only. Consult
recommended charts for navigation.

Spectacular snorkeling and diving on the reefs within Pelican Cay Land and Sea Park is the major attraction for visiting Sandy Cay.

A stretch of reef flanking the eastern shore of Sandy Cay represents one of the best destinations in Abaco for underwater exploration. Remarkable coral formations rise to the surface here with a myriad of underseas channels and cuts. Because fishing and spearing is strictly outlawed in the park boundaries, the fish life over the reef abounds.

Please observe these regulations. A great deal of effort and resources has gone into the establish-

ment of Abaco snorkeling and diving preserves.

NAVIGATION

Several mooring buoys are anchored near the reef. These are designated for boats under 25-foot. Larger boats should anchor, but never over the reef. This is prohibited and fines can be stiff.

When anchoring beyond the reef perimeter, post a watch on the bow to keep a sharp eye for coral formations before dropping the hook... and then only over sand.

An alternative and favorite choice for most boaters is to anchor to the west between Sandy Cay and Cornish Cay. In any unsettled weather, this is recommended as a day anchorage. Holding is fair in several feet of water. During periods of low water, it may be difficult to distinguish the separation between the two cays. A shoal spans the gap between the two cays.

From the anchorage, it is a short dinghy ride to the reef and mooring buoys. This is often a crowded destination, and moorings may be limited. Boaters are urged to take a line from other visitors and string their craft along from bow-to-stern. Courtesy and sharing are key words.

ASHORE

Sandy Cay is interesting to explore. There are rocky beaches and the pine-lined shores provide shade for picnics and relaxing. Sea bird life is abundant, and wading the clear, shallow flats will reveal all sorts of discoveries.

While Sandy Cay is accessible by smaller boats such as rentals, visitors should be especially aware of sea conditions offshore. The area is partially exposed to the ocean, and large swells moving inshore can affect anchoring or mooring. Likewise, this is why the area is recommended as a day anchorage.

LYNYARD CAY

Sand Bank

To Little
Harbour

BRIDGES CAY
(Private)

LYNYARD CAY

ATLANTIC OCEAN

NOT TO BE USED FOR NAVIGATION
Use as a reference only. Consult
recommended charts for navigation.

the southern section. The western shores of Lynyard are mostly well-protected from the effects of ocean swells.

ASHORE

The property ashore is private and there are a number of homes on the island. Beaches dot the western shoreline and are accessible by dinghy. Note there may be some areas that are posted off-limits. Respect the property owners' rights, and leave the scene as tidy as you found it. In calm weather you will find excellent snorkeling in the area of Goole Cay.

If you are piloting a vessel beyond the draft limitations of visiting Little Harbour, Lynyard Cay anchorages are a short dinghy ride to this popular destination.

Another view of Lynyard Cay taken from the south.

LYNYARD
CAY

Shoals

GOOLE
CAY

Towards the southern portion of Lynyard Cay are coves which provide excellent anchorages with good protection from most wind directions. The exception would be strong westerlies.

These anchorages are excellent stop-overs if you are transiting to or from points south, such as the Exumas, Eluthera or the Berry Islands. The anchorages are near passes into the ocean. Little Harbour Bar pass is at the northern tip of Lynyard Cay, and the ocean pass through Little Harbour Bay is just to the south.

Treat these passes with a great deal of respect

during times of heavy offshore seas. In most cases, breaking seas are usually visible over the bars. Keep an especially sharp lookout if they are not easily seen. Depths are in the 15-20 foot range through the passages proper.

NAVIGATION

Entrance into the Lynyard Cay anchorages is straightforward. Water depths in the anchorage to the north at the widest section of the island are in the 5 foot range. You can carry an average of 10 feet of water reasonably close to the beaches in

LITTLE HARBOUR, GREAT ABACO

BIGHT OF OLD ROBINSON

⚓

Tom Curry Point

Marked Channel

LITTLE HARBOUR ⚓

Hurricane Hole

Pete's Pub

Johnston Gallery / Studio

NOT TO BE USED FOR NAVIGATION
Use as a reference only. Consult
recommended charts for navigation.

Little Harbour is one of the most unique and remote ports of call in Abaco. Tucked away between rugged cliffs and high bluffs, this tiny community and harbour has escaped the development boom that so many of the other islands in the Abaco chain are experiencing.

NAVIGATION

The entrance to Little Harbour is a well-marked channel over a shallow bar. Reportedly, the depth is approximately 3-5 feet MLW. Boats with deeper draft should wait on a rising tide or high tide, which should provide depths in the 5-foot range. Inside, you can choose to anchor, or grab one of moorings (for a fee) provided by Pete's Pub.

ASHORE

Because it is secluded and largely pristine, this destination is especially popular with cruising boaters. Besides the beauty of the surroundings and the spectacular cresent-shaped beach, there are other attractions which draw visitors from throughout Abaco. One of the foremost is the Johnston's Gallery. Here works are featured by a highly acclaimed sculptor, Randolph Johnston, who passed away in 1992 after residing and working in Little Harbour for nearly a half century. His son, Pete, has carried on the tradition, sculpting unique bronze marine works and gold jewelry. Pete's, his father's and other island artists' works are displayed in the gallery. It's a worthwhile visit, and the history surrounding the Johnston family at Little Harbour is intriguing.

Equally enjoyable is Pete's Pub. This rustic, outdoor pub and restaurant is a favorite among seasoned cruisers and new visitors to Abaco alike. You can always count on meeting colorful characters here and listening to a variety of tales while saddled up to this open-air bar. Count on plenty of action on weekends with pig roasts, other special meals and entertainment on tap.

Another alternative is to anchor in nearby Bight of Old Robinson or at Lynyard Cay, and dingy into the harbor.

The Bight of Old Robinson itself offers numerous anchorage possibilities, as well as interesting dingy exploration.

Blow holes a short walk from Pete's Pub.

Scotland Cay